The Ashanti people have this old saying:
"Even a king needs a friend."
In a way back time, in a faraway land,
there lived the great king Amadou. The king
had everything he needed. But most of all,
he wanted a good friend.

"If I were not your king, would you still be my friends?" Amadou asked the people who worked for him.

"How can you even ask that?" said all the people around him.

"Long live Amadou!" they all shouted.

"Soon I will find out," Amadou thought.

One morning before the sun came up, Amadou quietly left the Great House. No one saw him leave. No one would ever know that it was King Amadou, because he looked like a poor man.

Before long, Amadou saw the boy who brought cooking oil to the Great House every day.

"Where are you going?" Amadou asked.

"To see the king," said the boy.

"What do you think of your king?" Amadou asked.

"Well, he's all right, but he laughs too much!" the boy said. Then he quickly ran away.

Amadou was surprised. He worked very hard, but he also liked to have a good laugh. He sat under a big tree to think.

Before long, the king's cook came by.

"Where are you going?" Amadou asked.

"To see the king," said the cook.

"Tell me, what do you think of your king?" Amadou asked.

"Well, he's all right," said the cook. "But he takes too long to eat, because he tells so many jokes."

Amadou was even more surprised. "I do like to take my time eating," he thought. "And I do tell jokes while I eat. But I always thought people liked them."

The king came to the house where the man who made pots lived.

"That is a great pot you are making," said Amadou. "It must be for your king."

"No," said the man. "I will keep this one for myself."

Then he pulled out another pot and said,
"I'll give this one to the king."

"But that one is not nearly as good,"
said Amadou.

"The king will never notice," said the man.
"He never even looks at the pots that he eats
from. All he ever does is tell jokes!"

Amadou was sad. "I guess I do tell too many jokes," he thought. "But isn't there one person who likes me the way I am? Isn't there one person that I can call a friend?"

Then it started to rain. A man called out, "Come in quickly, and get out of the rain."

Amadou went inside the man's small house. "My name is Lipo," said the man. "You are wet, and you must be cold. I'll boil some water and give you something warm to drink."

"Thank you," said Amadou, "but I can't pay you for it."

"I don't want any pay," said Lipo.

Lipo gave Amadou the warm drink.

"Now, have something to eat with me," said Lipo. "I have more than enough."

They started eating. "Eat more!" said Lipo. Then they started telling jokes. Amadou laughed with joy. He had never been so happy.

Soon the rain stopped.

"Before I go," said Amadou, "tell me, would you be as kind to your king?"

"I was happy to have you. I would also be excited if the king came here," said Lipo. "But the Great Amadou would not need a friend as poor as I am."

"Is that what you think?" Amadou laughed. "Well, I have something to tell you. I am your king! At last, I have found a friend who likes me the way I am."

Amadou asked Lipo to stay with him in the Great House. Lipo did not want to give up his small house, but the king came often to eat with his good friend. Hour after hour, they sat and told jokes. And Amadou laughed and laughed with joy.